TEC

SandCastle 2

Blends

sh

Carey Molter

ABDO
Publishing Company

Published by SandCastle™, an imprint of ABDO Publishing Company, 4940 Viking Drive, Edina, Minnesota 55435.

Printed in the United States.

Cover and interior photo credits: Corbis Images, Eyewire Images, FPG International, PhotoDisc.

Library of Congress Cataloging-in-Publication Data

Molter, Carey, 1973-
     Sh / Carey Molter.
       p. cm. -- (Blends)
     Includes index.
     ISBN 1-57765-412-9
      1. Readers (Primary) [1. English language--Phonetics.] I. Title. II. Blends (Series)

PE1119 .M65 2000
428.1--dc21

00-033207

The SandCastle concept, content, and reading method have been reviewed and approved by a national advisory board including literacy specialists, librarians, elementary school teachers, early childhood education professionals, and parents.

Let Us Know

After reading the book, SandCastle would like you to tell us your stories about reading. What is your favorite page? Was there something hard that you needed help with? Share the ups and downs of learning to read. We want to hear from you! To get posted on the Abdo Publishing Company Web site, send us email at:

sandcastle@abdopub.com

About SandCastle™

Nonfiction books for the beginning reader

- Basic concepts of phonics are incorporated with integrated language methods of reading instruction. Most words are short, and phrases, letter sounds, and word sounds are repeated.

- Readability is determined by the number of words in each sentence, the number of characters in each word, and word lists based on curriculum frameworks.

- Full-color photography reinforces word meanings and concepts.

- "Words I Can Read" list at the end of each book teaches basic elements of grammar, helps the reader recognize the words in the text, and builds vocabulary.

- Reading levels are indicated by the number of flags on the castle.

Look for more SandCastle books in these three reading levels:

Level 1
(one flag)

Level 2
(two flags)

Level 3
(three flags)

Grades Pre-K to K
5 or fewer words per page

Grades K to 1
5 to 10 words per page

Grades 1 to 2
10 to 15 words per page

sh

Shana thinks every day should be full of fun.

sh

Shane shivers in the shower of water.

His sister smiles.

sh

Shannen shapes the
sand with her shovel.

sh

Shawn likes being pushed on the swing in the shade.

sh

Shawna makes a funny fish face.

She is not shy.

sh

Sheri likes to help Sheridan.

She shows him the words.

sh

These pals share the paint.

They have their own brushes.

sh

We have fun when
we rush to brush our
teeth.

sh

What does Sasha like to wash and make shiny?

(dishes)

Words I Can Read

Nouns

A noun is a person, place, or thing

day (DAY) p. 5
face (FAYSS) p. 13
fun (FUHN) pp. 5, 19
paint (PAYNT) p. 17
sand (SAND) p. 9
shade (SHAYD) p. 11

shovel (SHUHV-uhl) p. 9
shower (SHOU-er) p. 7
sister (SISS-tur) p. 7
swing (SWING) p. 11
teeth (TEETH) p. 19
water (WAW-tur) p. 7

Plural Nouns

A plural noun is more than one
person, place, or thing

brushes (BRUHSH-ez)
  p. 17
dishes (DISH-ez) p. 21

pals (PALZ) p. 17
words (WURDZ) p. 15

Proper Nouns

A proper noun is the name
of a person, place, or thing

Sasha (SASH-A) p. 21
Shana (SHAY-nuh) p. 5

Shane (SHAYNE) p. 7
Shannen (SHAN-en) p. 9

22

Shawn (SHAWN) p. 11
Shawna (SHAWN-uh)
  p. 13

Sheri (SHAIR-ee) p. 15
Sheridan (SHAIR-i-duhn)
  p. 15

Verbs

A verb is an action or being word

be (BEE) p. 5
being (BEE-ing) p. 11
brush (BRUHSH) p. 19
does (DUHZ) p. 21
have (HAV) pp. 17, 19
help (HELP) p. 15
is (IZ) p. 13
like (LIKE) p. 21
likes (LIKESS) pp. 11, 15
make (MAKE) p. 21
makes (MAKESS) p. 13

pushed (PUSHT) p. 11
rush (RUHSH) p. 19
shapes (SHAYPSS) p. 9
share (SHAIR) p. 17
shivers (SHIV-urs) p. 7
should (SHUD) p. 5
shows (SHOHZ) p. 15
smiles (SMILEZ) p. 7
thinks (THINGKSS) p. 5
wash (WASH) p. 21

Adjectives

An adjective describes something

every (EV-ree) p. 5
fish (FISH) p. 13
full (FUL) p. 5
funny (FUH-nee) p. 13
her (HUR) p. 9
his (HIZ) p. 7

our (OUR) p. 19
own (OHN) p. 17
shiny (SHYE-nee) p. 21
shy (SHYE) p. 13
their (THAIR) p. 17
these (THEEZ) p. 17

23

Match these sh Words to the Pictures

shell

ship

shoes

shirt